Animals in the Wild

Elephant

by Mary Hoffman

Raintree Childrens Books
Milwaukee
Belitha Press Limited • London

Elephants are the largest mammals that
live on land. When an elephant calf is born,
it looks small next to its mother. However,
it weighs about 200 pounds. It is about
three feet high at the shoulder.

A mother elephant carries her calf for twenty-one months before it is born. She usually has one calf at a time. She could have another calf in three more years. The calf drinks its mother's milk for five years.

One kind of elephant lives in Asia. Males
are called bulls. Females are cows. They
are about nine feet tall at the shoulder.
They have trunks with one point and tusks.

The other kind of elephant lives in Africa. African bulls are larger than Asian elephants. They have bigger ears and tusks. Their trunks end in two points.

Elephants have two close relatives. One is
the hyrax. Hyraxes live in Africa, in rocky
holes. The parts of the two animals that
are most similar are the feet.

The other relative of the elephant is the
sea cow. Sea cows live in the water and are
very timid. Their teeth are like elephants'
teeth, and some of them have tusks.

Elephants live in the wild where the
weather is warm. In Asia, they live in
forests and in swamps.

In Africa, elephants live on the grasslands.
When the weather is too warm, elephants
flap their ears to help them cool off.

Elephants eat up to 600 pounds of food
each day. They use their trunks to feed
themselves plants like tree bark and grasses.

Elephants use their tusks to dig for salt
and to make holes to find water. People
kill elephants just for their ivory tusks.

Elephants use their trunks to help them to
drink. First an elephant sucks in over a
gallon of water. Then it squirts the water
into its mouth. Elephants drink about fifty
gallons a day.

Elephants also squirt water over
themselves and others in order to bathe.
They are good swimmers. They need to be
near a lot of water because they drink so
much and because they enjoy swimming.

Elephants roll in mud. When the mud covers
their skin, flies and other insects will not
bother them. The mud bath makes an
elephant's skin look like the color of mud.
Herds of thirty to forty take baths together.

Elephants are usually peaceful. But two
times a year bulls get excited easily. They
will charge anything that makes them
angry. The rest of the year, most elephants
are friendly and even playful.

Elephants are very smart animals. In Asia, elephants are treated with respect. They are trained to haul people, pull down trees, and drag or carry heavy loads.

African elephants are work animals, too. They are harder to train than Asian elephants. African laws protect elephants from hunters who want their ivory tusks.

First published in this edition in the United States of America 1984 by
Raintree Publishers Limited Partnership, 310 West Wisconsin Avenue,
Milwaukee, Wisconsin 53203.

Library of Congress Number: 84-15119

First published in the United Kingdom under the title
Animals in the Wild—Elephant
by Windward, an imprint owned by W H Smith Ltd., St. John's
House, East Street, Leicester LE1 6NE, by arrangement with
Belitha Press Ltd.

Text and illustrations in this form © Belitha Press 1983
Text © Mary Hoffman 1983

Dedicated to Dinshaw Malegamwala

Scientific Adviser: Dr. Gwynne Vevers
Picture Researcher: Stella Martin
Designer: Julian Holland

Acknowledgements are due to Bruce Coleman Ltd
for all photographs in this book with the following
exceptions: Jacana Ltd pp 4, 8-9; ZEFA Picture Library
p 14.

ISBN 0-8172-2408-4 (U.S.A.)

Library of Congress Cataloging in Publication Data

Hoffman, Mary, 1945—
    Elephant.

    (Animals in the wild)
    Summary: Shows the elephant in its natural
surroundings and describes its life and struggle
for survival.
    1. Elephants—Juvenile literature [1. Elephants]
I. Title. II. Series.
QL737.P98H584   1984   599.6'1   84-15119
ISBN 0-8172-2408-4

Printed in Hong Kong

4 5 6 7 8 9   93 92 91 90 89